SO-ACI-276

AMERICAN HISTORY BY DECADE

The

1950s

Titles in the American History by Decade series are:

The 1900s
The 1910s
The 1920s
The 1930s
The 1940s
The 1950s
The 1960s
The 1970s
The 1980s
The 1990s

AMERICAN HISTORY BY DECADE

The
1950s

Deanne Durrett

KIDHAVEN
PRESS™

THOMSON
————✦————™
GALE

San Diego • Detroit • New York • San Francisco • Cleveland
New Haven, Conn. • Waterville, Maine • London • Munich

THOMSON
————*————™
GALE

© 2004 by KidHaven Press. KidHaven Press is an imprint of The Gale Group, Inc., a division of Thomson Learning, Inc.

KidHaven™ and Thomson Learning™ are trademarks used herein under license.

For more information, contact
KidHaven Press
27500 Drake Rd.
Farmington Hills, MI 48331-3535
Or you can visit our Internet site at http://www.gale.com

LIBRARY OF CONGRESS CATALOGING-IN-PUBLICATION DATA

Durrett, Deanne, 1940–
  The 1950s / by Deanne Durrett.
    p. cm. — (American History by Decade)
Summary: Discusses the 1950s including music, integration, television, and the polio vaccine.
Includes bibliographical references (p.   ) and index.
  ISBN 0-7377-1747-5 (alk. paper)
1. United States—History—1945–1953—Juvenile literature. 2. United States—History—1953–1961—Juvenile literature. 3. Nineteen fifties—Juvenile literature. [1. United States—History—1945–1953. 2. United States—History—1953–1961. 3. Nineteen fifties.]. II. Title: Nineteen fifties. II. Title. III. Series.
  E813.D87 2004
  973.92—dc22
                                                          2003013327

Printed in the United States of America

Contents

CHAPTER ONE

Rock and Roll and the Teen Culture

The teenagers of the 1950s were born in the 1930s and 1940s. Their parents had seen hard times—the Great Depression and World War II. In the 1950s, the U.S. economy was in good shape. Now that times were good, these parents wanted their children's lives to be easier than theirs had been. And that is what happened. The 1950s was the best decade yet for teenagers. The birth of rock and roll changed music and teen life. By the end of the decade, teenagers were a segment of society with their own culture, style, spending money, and music.

1950s Music

Before the arrival of rock and roll, people of all ages listened to the same music. Musical categories included pop (popular), country, and rhythm and blues. While music was for all ages, it was, however, primarily divided into two segments—music for whites and music for blacks. Most radio disc jockeys thought that white audiences would not listen to black singers. Unfortunately, music (and much of American society) was segregated. This all began to change when an eighteen-year-old white boy sang music that sounded black. His name was Elvis Presley.

Elvis Presley

Elvis Presley's first recordings "That's When Your Heartache Begins" and "That's All Right Mamma" were not well received. Radio disc jockeys thought Elvis was black and refused to play his records.

Elvis's style was new. It was a mix of blues and country with a hint of gospel. In fact, Elvis Presley took black and

Sources: Bureau of Labor Statistics; Kingwood College Library; *National Vital Statistics Reports*, vol. 51, no. 3; U.S. Census Bureau.

Then and Now

	1950	2000
U.S. population:	151,684,000	281,421,906
Life expectancy:	Female: 71.1 Male: 65.6	Female: 79.5 Male: 74.1
Average yearly salary:	$2,992	$35,305
Unemployment rate:	5.3%	5%

Elvis sings and swivels his hips. Teenagers loved the rock star, but parents thought he was a bad influence.

white music, added his own style, and mixed it into a new creation.

Some people did not like Elvis or his style of music. They did not believe rock and roll belonged in their music world. For example, Sam Phillips of Sun Records booked Elvis Presley to perform at Grand Ole Opry for a month. Elvis was canceled after the first night. They said he was not singing country music the right way.

The fans, however, liked Elvis and his music. He became a star in January 1956 when "Heartbreak Hotel" took the top spot on the country and pop charts as well as the second spot on the rhythm and blues chart.

Through the 1950s Elvis Presley had continuous hits. His gold records in the 1950s (the songs with over a million sales) include "Heartbreak Hotel," "Love Me Tender," "Don't Be Cruel," "Hound Dog," and "I Was the One." Elvis's records continued to sell years after his death. Since the beginning of his career, fifty-one singles have reached gold or platinum status by today's standards (five hundred thousand for gold and 1 million for platinum). Many have sold several million copies.

Elvis made television appearances, starred in movies, and went on concert tours. He had a style that many people, especially parents, considered too sexy. When he performed, he swiveled his hips to the beat. The third time Elvis appeared on the *Ed Sullivan Show* (a variety television program) the cameraman had orders to stay focused above Presley's waist.

His style earned him the nickname "Elvis the Pelvis." This worried parents and made teenagers want to see Elvis even more. Teens flocked to his live concerts.

Bill Haley and His Comets

Hollywood musicals had always been a venue for reaching audiences. The 1950s were no exception, but different types

Bill Haley (center) and His Comets perform "Rock Around the Clock." The song became an instant hit when it was featured in a popular movie.

of movies, including dramas, featured rock and roll, making instant hits of bands and their songs. In 1955, for example, Bill Haley and His Comets' song "Rock Around the Clock" was used as the theme song for *Blackboard Jungle*—a movie set in a tough inner-city school. This was one of the first movies about teenagers and their problems created especially for a teenage audience.

The film focused on juvenile delinquency and rebellious teen leaders in a multiracial setting. *Blackboard Jungle* was a shocking film in its time. Several cities banned the movie because of its racial content. Others banned it fearing that it would spark violence. Where the movie was shown, teenagers flocked to see it. They loved the story about difficult teens and they loved the music.

The film and "Rock Around the Clock" were instant hits and so were Bill Haley and His Comets. The group had two more big hits, "Shake Rattle and Roll" and "See You Later Alligator." Both records reached a million in sales the first month after release.

Rock and Roll Pioneers

Other rock and roll pioneers included Jerry Lee Lewis as well as black singers such as Chuck Berry and Little Richard.

Jerry Lee Lewis stood at the piano, pounded out a rhythm, and sang "Whole Lotta Shakin' Goin' On" and "Great Balls of Fire!" These hits captured the top spot on all three music charts—pop, country, and rhythm and blues.

Rock stars such as Elvis and Lewis broke down the barriers between black and white music. Teens were more receptive to black singers. Little Richard had a wild style. His best known hits were "Tutti Frutti" and "Long Tall Sally." Guitar player Chuck Berry's hits included "Sweet Little Sixteen" and "Johnny B. Goode." The lyrics of Chuck Berry's songs went directly to the teenage heart. Teen acceptance led to millions of dollars in sales for these black artists. Teens' money talked, and businesses began to listen and cater to their tastes.

The Teen Culture

The Fabulous Fifties was the decade of the teen. Times were good and families did not need income from their children to survive. For the first time in history teens had money and time for fun. Most of them had part-time jobs or allowances for spending money. This money was used to buy clothing, music, and food.

Teens gathered at local **mom and pop** soda shops and diners (there were no chain fast-food restaurants). Teens ate the same type of foods they do today—hamburgers, hot dogs, and fries. Malts, shakes, and ice-cream sodas, however, were more popular than colas. While they enjoyed these treats, they listened to the jukebox. Most jukeboxes played one

Chuck Berry performs onstage. Teenagers of the 1950s accepted black artists.

A teenager selects a song on a jukebox. Jukeboxes were popular with teens throughout the 1950s.

song for a nickel and three for a dime. As soon as rock and roll selections became available, places with jukeboxes became popular with teens.

Besides listening to the jukebox, teenagers bought and collected seven-inch black vinyl records that played at the speed of 45 rpm (revolutions per minute). These 45s had one song on each side. Some record shops had booths where teens could listen to new records before making a purchase. For the most part, however, teens bought songs they heard on the radio and wanted to hear more often.

Many teenagers listened to their favorite music at home on a record player.

Listening to records in the 1950s was not as convenient as listening to CDs or MP3s today. The records were played on portable phonographs (record players) about the size of a small suitcase. These phonographs were not battery powered, so the records could only be enjoyed near an electrical outlet. Consequently, the portable phonograph was no more convenient than the radio. However, it offered a way to display a teen's record collection and to choose the songs to play.

Teens who listened to rock and roll liked the "Elvis look." Boys who wanted to be "cool cats" turned up the collars of their black leather motorcycle jackets and grew sideburns. They greased their hair and swept the sides back in a ducktail. (On special occasions, such as weddings and funerals, teen boys dressed like their fathers in suits and ties.)

Girls had their own fashion, too. Hairstyles included curly bangs with ponytails. In the late 1950s some girls wore short haircuts with **finger waves**. They favored sweaters with jeans or skirts. The skirts were long with hems at mid-calf. Almost every girl had a felt circle skirt with a poodle embroidered on it. Girls wore black and white saddle shoes or penny loafers with bobby socks. (Sometimes, however, for an adult event such as church or a wedding, teen girls dressed like their mothers in dresses with hats, gloves, and high heels.)

Sock Hops

Events were sponsored for teens, as they are now. Most schools held dances in the gym. (Some schools in the Bible Belt did not allow dances.) They called these dances sock hops because the students were required to remove their shoes to protect the gym floor.

Teens created new dances such as the bop and the stroll to fit the rock and roll beat. The most popular dance, however, was a form of jitterbug. The couple held hands and danced away and then together, stepping and tapping to the beat. They repeated this back and forward pattern. When the timing seemed right, the boy pulled the girl to his side. They loosed hands, slipped past each other, and clasped hands again. They then repeated the first pattern. The couple continued these steps and moves until the song ended.

Sock hops were dances held in the school gym. Teens had to remove their shoes to protect the gym floor.

People still go to sock hops to dance to 1950s music. They still enjoy 1950s movies on TV or rented VCR tapes. This decade is well remembered by those who lived it and much of it has been preserved for later generations to enjoy.

CHAPTER TWO

Integration

At the beginning of the 1950s some states had laws that segregated people by race. In the southern states black and white children did not go to school together. Schools for blacks were sometimes far away from their homes, but whites attended schools in their own neighborhoods, usually within a few blocks of their homes. This was legal. States could have "separate but equal" schools for blacks and whites.

Separate and Unequal

Unfortunately, the schools for blacks were seldom equal to the white schools in the area. The buildings were often run-down, supplies were usually short, the textbooks were outdated, and funding was low. Even when the building, supplies, and books were equal, the effort needed to attend a black school could make it unequal. For example, first grader Linda Brown lived in Topeka, Kansas. She had to cross a railroad **switchyard** and then ride a bus two miles to the nearest black elementary school. Linda's parents worried about this dangerous route to school. They tried to enroll her at the elementary school in their neighborhood. The black child, however, was not allowed to attend the white school.

Brown v. Board of Education

Linda's situation became the basis for a groundbreaking lawsuit that went all the way to the U.S. Supreme Court in 1952.

Linda Brown (center, front) had to cross a railroad yard and ride
a bus two miles to attend the closest all-black school.

In May 1954 the Court ruled that separate but equal was unconstitutional and that black children could attend white schools. This is called **integration**.

Some schools followed the law and enrolled all students who lived in the district. Others made plans to integrate over a period of time. The Little Rock, Arkansas, school district, for example, planned to begin integrating its Central High School in September 1957. Nine black students were selected to enroll at the school that fall.

Sitting on the steps of the Supreme Court in 1954, a woman holds a newspaper that announces the Court's ruling in *Brown v. Board of Education*.

Little Rock 1957

In the summer of 1957 people who opposed integration organized to try to stop the enrollment of the nine black students. Protesters from other cities joined the local people in filing a lawsuit they hoped would prevent integration of the school.

When this failed in the courts, Arkansas governor Orval Faubus called out the Arkansas National Guard to surround the school on opening day. Faubus claimed that the National Guard was needed to prevent violence.

Threats of violence delayed the enrollment of the nine students for three weeks. During this time about one thousand protesters stayed in the area outside the school. On September 23 the nine students tried to attend the school again. The crowd outside the school became unruly and police moved the nine students to a safer place.

The next day Little Rock mayor Woodrow Mann asked for federal assistance in integrating the school. In response, President Dwight Eisenhower sent one thousand army troops to Little Rock. In addition, army officers took command of ten thousand Arkansas National Guardsmen. On September 24, 1957, U.S. Army troops escorted the nine black students into Little Rock Central High School, and the first integrated class graduated from Central High in 1959.

Years would pass, however, before school integration would be complete in American schools. Still, school integration was the first step in gaining civil rights for blacks. The next step would bring segregation before the Court again and introduce the nation to Rosa L. Parks, Martin Luther King Jr., and civil rights.

Rosa L. Parks

In the early 1950s segregation laws in Montgomery, Alabama, required blacks to ride in the back of public buses.

U.S. Army troops escort black students to school in Little Rock, Arkansas, in 1959.

About two-thirds of Montgomery bus riders were black. Only five rows of seats, however, were reserved for these passengers. And if a white rider needed a seat, a black person had to stand and give up one of these few seats.

On December 1, 1955, Rosa L. Parks was asked to give her seat to a white passenger. She quietly refused. The police were called and Parks was arrested but freed on bail that night. Some reports said that she refused to move because she was tired. Others thought she might have planned to get arrested. Parks later explained that she was tired of the way she and her people were treated. She wrote in her book, "Our mistreatment was just not right, and I was tired of it."[1] She went on to explain, "I did not get on the bus to get arrested. I got on the bus to go home."[2] The events that followed Parks's arrest, however, would change the nation.

Parks's case was used in a lawsuit that would bring the Alabama segregation laws before the U. S. Supreme Court.

Because Parks refused to give up her seat on the bus, Martin Luther King Jr. led the black population of Montgomery in a bus boycott that lasted 381 days until the U.S. Supreme Court ruled that segregated public transportation is unconstitutional.

Tired of the mistreatment of blacks, Rosa Parks refused to give up her seat to a white man on a public bus in 1955.

After Rosa Parks was arrested, Martin Luther King Jr. (center, right) led a bus boycott that lasted more than a year.

The civil rights movement that began in the 1950s with Rosa L. Parks and Martin Luther King Jr. would go on for years defeating one unjust law after another. Today there is no legal segregation and blacks have equal rights and equal opportunity under the law. It is illegal to discriminate against anyone because of race or skin color. Still, some people violate the rights of others. When they do, they can be punished by law.

CHAPTER THREE

Television Comes to the American Home

In the early days of television, cable companies, satellite dishes, and remote controls did not exist. Most families had only one television set. The screen was small by today's standards (fourteen to seventeen inches) and black and white. If a family received three channels, they were lucky. Still, 88 percent of all homes in the United States had a television set by 1955.

Changing Lifestyle

Television may have changed American life more than any other invention. When television reached the American home, viewing occupied much of the time once spent talking, reading, playing games, doing homework, and exercising. To accommodate almost constant viewing, many families moved meals from the dining table to the living room. As a result, individually packaged heat-and-serve meals called TV dinners became available in grocery stores. These meals were often served on TV trays—special foldaway trays large enough to hold the diner's plate, silverware, and glass.

About the time TV dinners made their debut, some city water companies noticed that increased water usage matched the timing of television commercials. This showed that many people adjusted their routine to fit television viewing. They took their bathroom breaks during commercials.

With this growing interest in television, the industry expanded rapidly to meet the demand and interests of viewers. Television stations sprang up in every city. By the end of the decade most people in urban areas could get good

A woman pulls a TV dinner from the freezer. These heat-and-serve meals were very popular in the 1950s.

reception on at least one station. Most large cities, how-ever, had three stations.

Along with local programming, each station linked with ABC, NBC, or CBS to broadcast network programs. This made it possible to broadcast the most popular shows nationwide during prime-time evening hours when the audience size was largest.

Favorite Shows

Television offered family entertainment plus shows aimed at each age level. Some of them are still shown on television as

By 1955 most American homes had a television set.

Actress Lucille Ball stars in a scene from *I Love Lucy*. Reruns of the immensely popular show still air today.

reruns and many of them are available on videotape or DVD. The popular family shows included *I Love Lucy, Ozzie and Harriet, Father Knows Best*, and *Leave It to Beaver*. Comedians Jack Benny, George Burns and Gracie Allen, and Milton Berle had their own shows. These shows included comedy skits with a regular cast and the comedian star plus a guest star.

The 1950s television show *Leave It to Beaver* was about a family with two boys, Wally and Beaver.

Variety shows hosted by Ed Sullivan, Bob Hope, and Jimmy Dean offered variety acts and introduced America to future stars. Late night viewers watched Steve Allen host the *Tonight Show* in 1954. Jack Paar began hosting the show in 1957. Fifty years after the first airing, Americans still enjoy the *Tonight Show with Jay Leno*.

Fifties programming aimed at children included *Howdy Doody*, a puppet with its human sidekick Buffalo Bob. Older children hurried home from school to see the *Mickey Mouse Club* with a regular cast of young stars called Mouseketeers.

Saturday morning adventure included *Sky King*, America's Favorite Flying Cowboy. Saturday morning viewers also enjoyed saddle-and-six-shooter Western stars including Gene Autry, Roy Rogers, and the Lone Ranger.

After school, teenagers watched Dick Clark and *American Band Stand*. Regular *Band Stand* teen dancers rated the latest

Television shows in the 1950s were created for every audience. *The Mickey Mouse Club* was designed to appeal to children.

rock and roll record releases and demonstrated the newest fast and slow dances. *American Band Stand* dancers introduced the stroll (a cross between a folk dance and modern line dancing).

Soap Operas

In the afternoons, the networks presented serial dramas called soap operas because they were usually sponsored by soap companies. Daily serials such as *The Guiding Light, As the*

In a 1954 scene from *The Guiding Light*, a nurse comforts a patient. *The Guiding Light* is still on the air today.

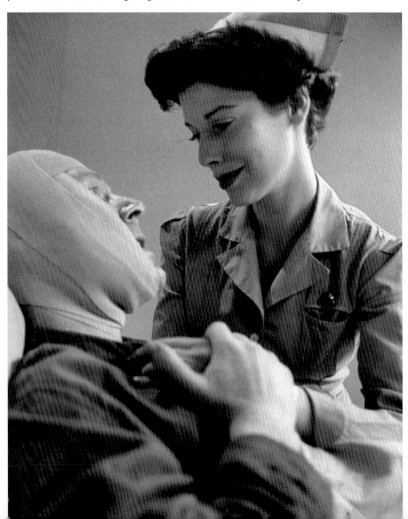

When Lucy and Ricky were expecting a baby on *I Love Lucy*, the cast was not allowed to use the word *pregnant*.

World Turns, and *The Edge of Night* were popular in the 1950s. These programs were designed to appeal to homemakers and modern versions of these programs are aired daily in the afternoon today.

These dramas presented the everyday life of the characters including their loves, hates, accomplishments, and mistakes—similar to soap operas today. In 1950s TV programming, however, life was presented as it should be, not how it actually was. None of the characters used bad words. Many of the realistic activities that are seen on television today were not allowed then. For example, married couples were always shown sleeping in twin beds. One season, Lucy and Ricky (the main characters on *I Love Lucy*) were expecting a baby. They were not allowed to use the word *pregnant* on the show.

Contestant Charles Van Doren (left) and host Jack Berry stand on the set of *Twenty-One*. A huge scandal erupted when the public learned that the show was fixed.

Scandal!

In addition to dramas and comedy, game shows were popular. These included *Concentration*, *Tic Tac Dough*, and *The Price Is Right* during the day. The prime-time quiz shows such as *The $64,000 Question* drew huge viewing audiences. The most popular contestants answered questions correctly week after week, increasing the value of their cash prize. *Twenty-One* (the winner earned twenty-one points by answering questions valued from one to eleven) topped the weekly ratings in 1957 when Charles Van Doren defeated the standing champion, Herbert Stempel. Van Doren continued on a fourteen-week winning streak that netted him $129,000.

Three years later an investigation of the quiz show ended in congressional hearings. During these hearings, Congress discovered that the producers of the quiz show controlled the outcome of the contests. Van Doren confessed to Congress that he was involved in rigging *Twenty-One*.

Van Doren and other contestants had been given the questions and answers before the show. The producers did this to entertain the audience and increase ratings. They considered this part of show business. Congress and most Americans, however, thought it was cheating. As a result, no quiz shows were produced for about twenty years.

During the 1950s television expanded rapidly and enjoyed overwhelming popularity. And it suffered growing pains along with the glory.

CHAPTER FOUR

Polio Conquered

I n the early 1950s a mysterious disease plagued America. Tragically, it mostly struck young children. No one knew how it spread, and there was no cure. People avoided crowds. Summer camps, public swimming pools, and movie theaters were closed while researchers worked frantically to find a vaccine to prevent the disease.

Almost fifty-eight thousand cases of polio were reported in the summer of 1952. This was the worst polio epidemic in U.S. history. Parents were gripped by fear that one of their children would be crippled for life or die from polio.

What Is Polio?

Paralytic poliomyelitis (polio) is a disease that attacks the nervous system and causes **paralysis**. Most polio victims are children.

The disease begins with flulike symptoms and most people recover in a few days. Some people, however, become gravely ill. This happens when the disease attacks the nerves in the spinal cord. One or all of the victim's limbs (arms and legs) can be **paralyzed**. In the worst cases, the virus attacks the nerves that control breathing and swallowing. These victims are likely to die. In the 1950s a machine that helped the paralyzed victim breathe offered the only hope.

A physical therapist helps two children with polio. Most polio
victims were children.

Iron Lungs

This machine, called an iron lung, helped polio patients inhale and exhale. The patient is placed on a narrow bed and rolled into a machine that encloses the body up to the neck. Once the doors are closed, the iron lung becomes a sealed

A young polio patient breathes with the aid of an iron lung.

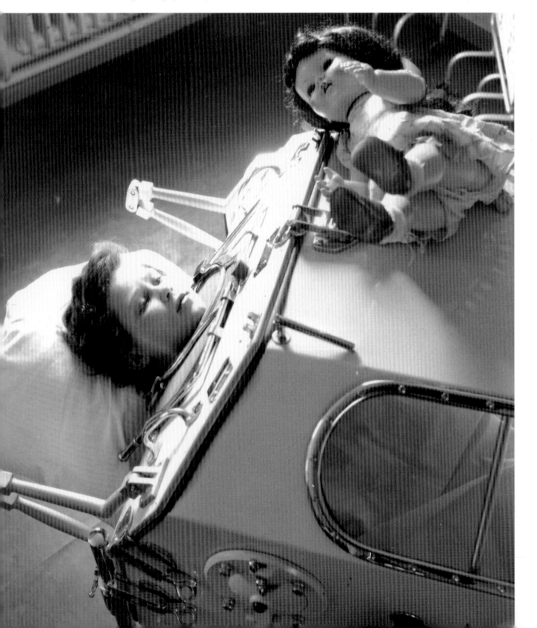

chamber. Only the patient's head remains outside the coffin-like canister. The iron lung performs mechanical artificial respiration by increasing and decreasing air pressure against the patient's chest. Increased pressure forces air from the patient's lungs. Decreased pressure pulls air into the patient's lungs.

During a polio **epidemic**, hospital wards were lined with polio victims encased in iron lungs. The whish of the iron lung became a normal hospital sound.

Treatment

When the polio virus attacks the nerves that control the arms and legs, the affected limb withers and bends. Early treatments involved placing the deformed, paralyzed limbs in casts and splints. With no exercise the muscles of the paralyzed limb weakened further. In fact, this treatment did more harm than good. Some victims underwent many surgeries in an effort to correct extreme deformities. Still, many children who were victims of polio lived the rest of their lives with one or more deformed or paralyzed limbs.

By the 1950s, however, an Australian army nurse, Elizabeth Kenny, had brought a new treatment for polio victims to the United States. This treatment helps strengthen weakened muscles. As the result, some victims thought to be hopeless walked again.

The treatment involves applying moist hot packs to stiff muscles and exercising those muscles. Trained nurses would massage and **flex** the patient's paralyzed limbs. (Today we call this exercise physical therapy.) Forcing stiff joints to bend can be extremely painful. Still the weeks and months of pain were worth the effort for those victims who were able to walk again.

Long hospital stays, iron lungs, physical therapy, surgery, braces, and wheelchairs were expensive. Most families needed financial help when polio struck. And money was needed for research to find a way to prevent polio.

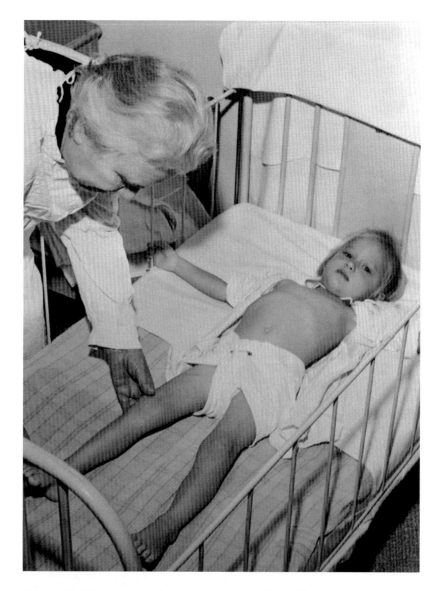

Elizabeth Kenny examines a young patient. Kenny's muscle treatment helped some polio victims to walk again.

March of Dimes

In 1938 President Franklin D. Roosevelt (a polio victim himself) created the National Foundation for Infantile Paralysis (NFIP) to raise money to fight polio. One of the NFIP volunteers, comedian Eddie Cantor, asked people to send dimes to President Roosevelt at the White House. Cantor called the flow of coins the "March of Dimes." The March of Dimes became an annual fund-raising event to fight polio.

By the 1950s research scientists had made many discoveries about the disease. They knew the disease was caused by

American Airlines flew this model of a polio vaccine bottle around the nation to collect money for the 1955 March of Dimes.

the poliovirus. They also knew that polio was caused by three types (strains) of the virus. And they knew that a successful polio vaccine would cause the human immune system to create antibodies to all three strains. Creating this vaccine, however, required a huge amount of time and hard

Young boys make faces as they receive polio vaccinations.

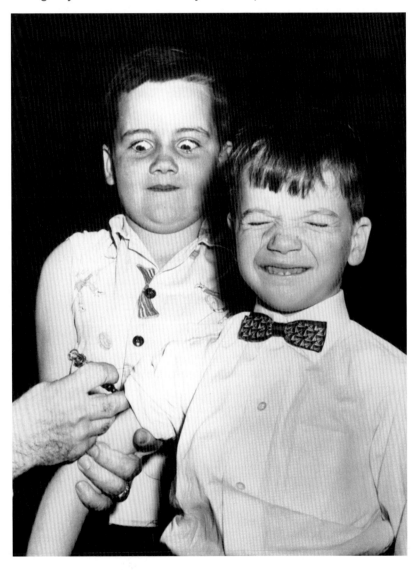

work. In addition, money was needed to buy laboratory space, equipment, supplies, and to pay the salaries of the researchers and their staffs.

Victory at Last!

In 1949 the NFIP chose researcher Jonas Salk to head its polio vaccine research program. By 1954 Salk had a vaccine ready to test on humans. Almost 2 million schoolchildren participated in the polio vaccine **field trials** (tests). And on April 12, 1955, the University of Michigan Polio Vaccine Evaluation Center declared the Salk vaccine "safe, effective and potent."[3] People soon began receiving polio vaccinations.

By the end of the decade more than 450 million doses of the vaccine had been used to prevent polio, and polio vaccination was added to routine childhood **immunizations**.

Polio was conquered in the United States and most other modern countries in the world in 1955. Swimming pools, movie theaters, and summer camps reopened. With polio conquered, the NFIP changed its name to the March of Dimes and went on to tackle birth defects and other health threats to children.

With the conquest of polio, the birth of rock and roll, advances in integration, and the growth of television, the fifties decade paved the way for the modern age and a better America.

Notes

Chapter Two: Integration

1. Rosa L. Parks, *Quiet Strength*. Grand Rapids, MI: Zondervan, 1994, p. 22.

2. Parks, *Quiet Strength*, p. 23.

Chapter Four: Polio Conquered

3. "March of Dimes Milestones and Timeline," 2003, March of Dimes. www.marchofdimes.com.

Glossary

epidemic: The rapid spread of a contagious disease.

field trials: A way to measure the effectiveness of a new medicine. Some participants are given the medicine and others are given a fake. Then the results are compared.

finger waves: Hair waves created by using the fingers to swirl wet, gelled hair to the right and then to the left. The crest of the wave is held in place with wave clamps until it dries.

flex: Bend.

immunizations: Vaccinations that cause the body to create antibodies to fight a specific disease.

integration: Bringing people of different races together.

mom and pop: A local couple who owns a neighborhood shop.

paralysis: The inability to move when damaged nerves cannot send messages from the brain to the muscles.

paralyzed: Cannot move.

segregated: Separated. Black and white students were not allowed to go to the same school.

switchyard: An area where railroad tracks can be moved to allow trains to switch tracks and go a different direction.

For Further Exploration

Books

Barry Denenberg, *All Shook Up: The Life and Death of Elvis Presley*. New York: Scholastic, 2001. This biography covers Elvis Presley's career and life from birth to death. It includes a look at his influence on teenagers and pop culture.

Peg Kehret and Denise Shanahan, *Small Steps: The Year I Got Polio*. Morton Grove, IL: Albert Whitman, 2000. In this book Peg Kehret shares her experience as a polio victim and survivor in the 1950s. She covers the sudden onset of the disease, diagnosis, treatment, and how it was to be a teenager dealing with polio.

Rock and Roll Generation: Teen Life in the 50s. Alexandria, VA: Time Life, 1999. This book is a pictorial history of teen life in the 1950s covering rock and roll, television, integration, polio, and much more.

Mildred Pitts Walter, *The Girl on the Outside*. New York: William Morrow, 1982. This novel gives an accurate account of life in 1957 Little Rock, Arkansas, as two teenage girls are caught in the strife of school integration.

Websites

The Fifties Web (www.fiftiesweb.com). This website covers television shows, music, Elvis, and fads of the fifties.

Little Rock Central High 40th Anniversary (www.central high57.org). This site has a page on the 1957–1958 school year and a time line of the integration of Little Rock Central High with photos.

March of Dimes (www.marchofdimes.com). This site covers the story of the conquest of polio with a history of the March of Dimes.

Time 100: Heroes & Icons (www.time.com). This site offers a profile of Rosa L. Parks, a few photos, plus quotes in Parks's voice.

Index

Picture Credits

Cover image: © Bettmann/CORBIS
© Bettmann/CORBIS, 8, 19, 21, 23, 38, 40
Centers for Disease Control and Prevention/Charles
   Farmer, 35
Alfred Eisenstaedt/Time Life Pictures/Getty Images, 16
© The Everett Collection, 10
© William Gottlieb/CORBIS, 25
© Hulton/Archive by Getty Images, 12, 31, 36
Carl Iwasaki/Time Life Pictures/Getty Images, 18
Chris Jouan, 7
© Harold M. Lambert/SuperStock, 26
Library of Congress, Prints & Photographs Division, LC-
   USZ62-107269, 39
Library of Congress, Prints & Photographs Division, LC-
   USZ62-111235, 22
© McFadden Publishing/CORBIS, 14
© Genevieve Naylor/CORBIS, 13
Photofest, 27, 28, 29, 32
Walter Sanders/Time Life Pictures/Getty Images, 30

About the Author

Deanne Durrett is the author of nonfiction books for readers from third grade through high school. She writes on many subjects and finds research and learning exciting. Durrett was a teenager in the 1950s, and she had fun writing this book. You can visit her website at www.deannedurrett.com.